# A BOY NAMED SASHA
## An International Adoption Story

by D.R. Now

DORRANCE PUBLISHING CO., INC.
PITTSBURGH, PENNSYLVANIA 15222

*All Rights Reserved*
Copyright © 2011 by D. R. Now
No part of this book may be reproduced or transmitted
in any form or by any means, electronic or mechanical,
including photocopying, recording, or by any information
storage and retrieval system without permission in
writing from the publisher.

ISBN: 978-1-4349-0753-0

Printed in the United States of America

*First Printing*

For more information or to order additional books, please contact:
Dorrance Publishing Co., Inc.
701 Smithfield Street
Pittsburgh, Pennsylvania 15222
U.S.A.
1-800-788-7654
*www.dorrancebookstore.com*
*www.dorrancebookstore.com*

*This book is dedicated to Aleksandr.*

*A story of how you became part of our family.*
*May you enjoy all of life's pleasures.*
*With all my love*
*MaMa*

**FAMILY FOREVER DAY**

Name: _____

We became a Family on: _____

Special Comments: _____
_____
_____
_____
_____
_____
_____
_____
_____
_____
_____


This book was given to you by: _____

Deep inside our hearts we knew

We had a special place for you.

Once the paperwork was done,

We waited for you, our new son.

While we waited, we prepared your room.

We hoped to bring you home really soon.

Then we got the call to see

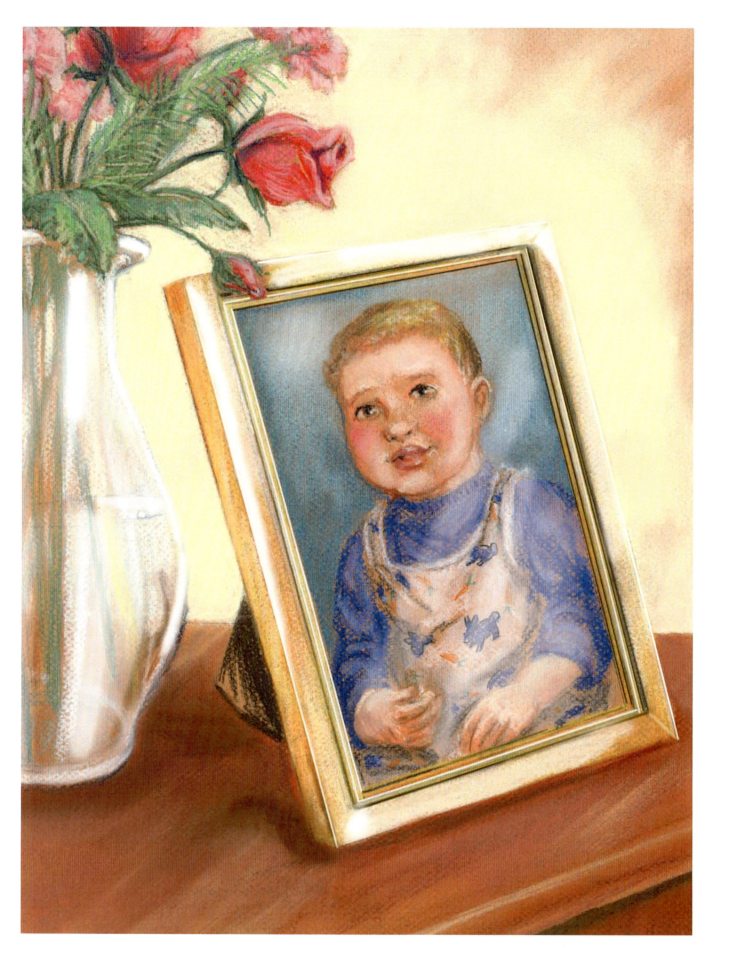

You, our son, our family.

The flight was booked, and the luggage was packed.

We came with clothes and toys and snacks.

Then we met you for the very first time.

You were scared at first, then things were fine.

We played.

We laughed.

We snacked together.

We even had a chance to enjoy the weather.

Finally, the moment had come
to go to court to make you our son.

Now the time to say goodbye
to caretakers and friends.

You were brave, and
you did not cry.

You took your first plane ride that day.

You were tired, but you couldn't wait to get home and play.

The trip was long, our energy zapped
and then HURRAY! You finally napped.

Now that you are truly home,
you have a family to call your own.

Don't ever forget our love for you.
It is something we want you to carry your whole life through.